The Truth a
You and Everyone Else

Deshna Jain

BookLeaf
Publishing

The Truth about Me, You and Everyone Else
© 2023 Deshna Jain

All rights reserved.

Deshna Jain asserts the moral right to be
identified as author of this work.

Presentation by *BookLeaf Publishing*

Web: www.bookleafpub.com

E-mail: info@bookleafpub.com

ISBN: 9789357212335

First edition 2023

ACKNOWLEDGEMENT

You know who you are and what you have done for me. Know now that I will be grateful forever.

The Act of Love

Let's dig claws into each other and peel each
other raw
Show me not just your naked self
But your vulnerable self
I want to see the color of your blood
I want to speak things into your ears and then
watch that blood rise to your cheeks
I want to touch your bones
I want to rearrange them, make love to them and
keep them warm
I want to see you from the inside
Make me your skin and I'll make you mine
And we can take care of each other when stars
shoot down on us
We'll burn together and then love some more
And laugh at the insanity of the universe as it
sizzles away on our skins
Let's tear each other apart and rebuild each other
together
I'll be your masterpiece and you'll be mine

Snow-White Smiles

Mirror mirror on the wall
Who's the happiest of them all?

Is it that scent I saved in a picture some years
ago?
When someone smiled and I wanted to
remember it,
When I saw a smile for the first time perhaps
that reached the eyes
And it was as if I'd witnessed a miracle
A story from a Disney movie unfolding in front
of me
It rouses a funny feeling in my heart
I feel that feeling tearing my eyes but my lips
don't turn up
I stand in front of you and try, mirror, have you
not seen me?

Is the happiest that smile that knows to shine in
the arms of many,
The one that stays on only the lips, it doesn't
know to travel to the eyes
And in that way, its beauty really only stays on
the surface

And even then the eyes, even when they don't
smile, laugh, such a foreign concept

My own shadows from 2 years ago sneaked into
my room
And asked me if it still hurt when I stood in front
of you, mirror, trying to feel what all the smiles
I'd known must have felt

I press my face with my hands, and pull at my
mouth
Why do I only see a scared little line of
something sad living in the moisture of my
irises?

Don't you see it, mirror? Can't you teach me?
Take me to the happiest smile, or just bring me
the recipe
I don't like feeling broken in my many happy
memories

X-Ray Vision

Don't look at me like you know me when you
take my naivete for compassion.
Don't smile at me as if you know my heart when
you take my self indulgence for introversion
Don't laugh with me on little things, it's not my
relief, it's my heinity
You see what you want to see, often a
hallucination, an absent beauty
You never see to really see, it's my arrogance,
not intrepidity
I often smile to ridicule, I'm never one to love
I'm never looking at silver linings, I'm just
mocking our curse
And when I cry - I almost don't - it's loathsome
beyond reproach.
Perhaps it's the charm of appearances - which
lies in their deception - or maybe it's savagery of
the highest order - one with no motive, just a
habit from practice for a reason I lost before I
could repress

Big Bear

Little bear little bear
What is it that you fear?
Is it the monster in the backyard or the one in
your head?

Little bear little bear
The whispers that you hear
You hear them for a reason you won't find under
your bed

Little bear little bear
Pressing your hands on your ears
Only works to block out the noise from outside

Little bear little bear
You can scream your heart here
It's okay, I won't tell how you cried

September

It's scary, September
When it brings change
No I'm not talking 'bout rain
September
Was when I first had my heart break
When the weather first changed in my heart
And when I realised things don't stay forever
I guess I should've seen the leaves fall closely
When they swiveled and fell loosely
I should've held one in my hand
And asked it how it felt
To love and then fall away
And everytime now that I stand
Under a lamppost
When it's blue in the air,
No I'm not talking 'bout the sky
September
When I first loved a girl
When I first loved myself
When I first loved the change that autumn meant
I don't want to start all over again
Can you meet me where we first did?
It's September
And I want to feel love again

Beloved

I met my beloved
On a stranded winter street
She had a wind like stride and a storm like glance
Yet she passed me by like a cool breeze
My beloved
She raised her arms as she walked under the trees to feel the leaves just like I did
She wore deep white scars on her back - to say she wasn't afraid of being broken
She kissed fractured smiles on me so I could do the same
My beloved
She knew I had seen her in pieces, I'd fallen
She knew I was drunk on a floating scent that night around that stranded winter street
My beloved, she talked about the charms of the world as if it was yet to break her
And laughed just like that, mocking the stars for not knowing me like she did
My beloved,
She loved me when I didn't, whenever I didn't
And yet talked about the foreignity of friendships and love

She knew the shortcomings of love and she
knew what scared me
She was a little wicked that way, my beloved
She knew how to tease me until I broke and then
to build me back up
All new
So when she touched me, I believed with all my
heart
She was my, only mine, and my only
Beloved

Asking to be loved

Slit it ever so slightly
My skin, it pricks when cut
You wanted to see me from within
My blood, my bones, my skin
Strange though,
I don't object when you dig in
Trying to find the "real" me

But let me tell you a secret
The marks on my face
Every wound you trace with your lips
So gently
Afraid to hurt me more
Is me
The pain that sat on my skin and left scars is me
The rough emboss where I patched up my skin is
me
You can dig as deep as you'd like
You'll only find yourself coming out the other
side
You see, I'm not an abyss
My eyes, not an ocean
I'm not a fairy tale,
My heart, not a rabbit hole
You won't find a wonderland

In this head of lost hopes
I'm not yours to save
I'm just a girl
Who asked to be loved
By you, by my mother, by every passing
stranger,
But mostly by me

Walk of shame

It bit into my skin like frost
I didn't feel it
I only laughed at it's fragile attempts to swoon
me into a fetish,
even though it's a tale often told;
There's never telling how quickly ice can settle
in your veins.
You only wake up one day, numb

I still laugh at the branches of trees in autumn
and cry out in winter out of jealousy.
They rebuild their happiness every season, a
talent I can never quite possess.
I sleep and I break some. I wake up and I break
some more.

This bitterness I live with, that comes from all
the sweet things that I cannot have,
The stubborn child inside hates it
It hates that it wasn't loved enough to love.
It hates that it never laughed enough and it hurts.
It hates the things it cannot have because of
things it never had.
This child saves me from shame.
Gives me someone to blame all my madness on.

And I shamelessly use the little innocence it has
left to hold my own wasted self straight.

Familiarity

She looks at me, "familiarity", sometimes
unthinkingly
And I dismiss it
Misinterpreting her silence
Misjudging her expression
Looking away, at another intense stare
That turns out to be a lost trail of thought that
ran right through me and into the walls
I stand because moving might mean I want to
talk
Except I do want to talk
Our eyes often meet with strangers, and
strangers offer comfort in their gaze,
So I lock my eyes with the strangest
These locked eyes don't see wistfulness, don't
see friendship, don't see the stretched out hands
of familiarity
Maybe because she has an old habit
She speaks in two voices
And the screech is sometimes louder than the
soothe
So my childish brain drinks away into newness
With the intention to keep it just that.

Wind

I enjoyed being the wind
I touched the mountains, I touched the sea
There were songs, feelings, laughter that I could
carry
I sang in the forests, the cities and the hills
I passed through open hair and windowsills

But I never knew, I could never expect
That if I touched you, I would never forget
That I'd carry your scent, and a strong sense of
longing
And then shake it away, trying to turn back

I became the wind to escape a memory
Now I've become one
I couldn't stop, couldn't stay,
I couldn't hold things, couldn't turn away
I tried to turn back but the wind doesn't.

I hated being the wind.

Color Palette

The water drops
On windowshops
Painting pictures of their own
Remaking the past, as if they've known
The colors and their secrets, the music in my
head
The laughter as it echoed, and the all the voices
that I dread
As I trace my fingers along to make sense of the
dew
I think of all the had beens of my formiddable
hues
Of the red that colors my lips in love
Of the anger, the fire, the spirit of my blood
Of the gray tones, the remnants of my fading
smiles
The ash, the waste that goes on for miles
I think the blue for the skies that were
The cottonseed breeze in an intensifying blur
I think the green for my whimsical rage
That makes home on my skin, makes my misery
my cage
I think of the pink and the happiness I had
The flush of my cheeks, I can no longer stand

And then I think of the black, the oblivion, the
end
The gravity of it as it pulls me back into the
blend
Of emotions, of all I thought I'd escaped
And I looked back to see all the borderless
shapes
I see me, I see you, I see a rainbow of the past
And I pull my hand out of that void
I swipe over the dew drops
On the windowshops, now won't let them speak
I'll love the colourlessness that brings with it a
silence so sweet

War story

You've worn your armor well
The creaks of dented metal as you move are
music to your ears
Bruises where the armor sunk in from impact -
you wear them like jewellery
It's a symbol, your armor. Of the battles you've
fought
You tell the tales of your glory
And you relish in the awes of your adulating
audience
Because no one really asks if you won the war
You say, "and this big scar I got when I fought
off the demon haunting the dark twilights under
my bed, waiting to grab my leg"
"And these claw marks are from the monsters
that my mind unleashed in early May, after Sky
cheated"
You see your audience bob their heads up and
down in rhythm with your words
They don't need to know if you still find it hard
to sleep without a night light
They don't need to know that you're struggling
to love again
People just love a good battle story

And you've had so many, that you put up a show
every people gathering, and boast a little more
everytime than the time before

A Witch's Curse

It was writ on his skin
For a smile to elude him
To chase after that same whisper -
An instruction to follow,
Never knowing who's
Never knowing why

He must've sinned
He must've thought
A witch's curse doesn't come for nothing
Is there a lesson to learn?
An epiphany that evades him?
That sense that he knew exactly what was
wrong, but didn't.
A sense that he knew exactly how to fix it, but
didn't.

The 'what' was parasitically predatory.
A half empty, half disdainful memory.
A chain of thought suffocatingly paradoxical
A prevaricate belief of a sin or perhaps a tragedy

The push and pull had done its work of wear
And continued ever so diligently to do it more
And yet you ask him what tired him of his wits
And drove him mad.

A Hundred Songs

Once upon my hundred lives
I promised you a hundred songs
And in each song, I told you
I'd give you my heart
But it's easier in songs,
When nothing goes my way
And yet we're still in love
Here, I have words in my head,
But promises on my lips that don't let me have
you
Or me
Or anyone else
Words that make me scream in pain.
I heard you cried
A hundred times
I saw you die a hundred lives
For a hundred lives, I've tried but
This rhapsody, I can only
Set into rhythms and sing

Rabbit Hole

Sometimes I fall asleep and I start falling
Down a rabbit hole, a spiral of my own
misgivings and my own secret thoughts
Good and bad
Tranquil and hurricane-like
Godly and perverted
Euphoric and tragic
Unfeeling and rhapsodic
All of them like a mesh around my brain
pushing and pulling in different directions
Like children trying to get your attention.
Like demons trying to snatch up on a piece of
godly meat.
I'm scared and happy and ecstatic and hopeless.
And waking up is no less of a hallucination.
No less of a nightmare.
No less of a dream.
And frankly, I'm too tired to fight.
So I close my eyes and let fall.

Me

Over the mountains and under the sea
I'm looking for something, I'm looking for me
Have you seen that smile, that's been gone a
while?
If you ever find it, give it back to me

If you ever find it, don't turn it around
I've heard it, I have. I don't like that sound
I'm looking I'm looking, I haven't yet found
I've toppled the mountains, I've dug up the
ground.

Up in the rain clouds and through the wet grass
I'm searching. I'm searching all the moments that
pass.
Have you seen that glow, that was here long
ago?
If you ever find it, trap it in a glass

If you ever find it, don't let it escape
It's a naughty little thing, you won't see it shift
shape
I know it, I know that one day I will find
That thing dear to me, that got lost in time

Witch Like Me

It began again
The curse of moonlight
One night
When I lived through a happy dream

I was a witch in my dream with love and
laughter and magic and -
Oh, tragic, how tragic it was to wake
And find myself on a stake
To feel my skin burn, my lungs break
Look for the tiniest sliver of hope and catch it
Can't catch it
I'm a witch, and
It's hope, not magic
"Hope comes from within", my dream had said
Hope from within, I lit when I went to bed

It died before I could when I smelled the smoke
And woke up to everyone I knew holding me
with ropes
The confusion, the betrayal, the anger, the
anguish
The screaming only I seemed to hear, the faces
that vanished

As ash flew up and covered my face, setting
ground for the flames to take over
Tried to shake myself out of it but then suddenly
felt sober
The case my mind fought of whether it's better
to live a villian or die a witch
Was there a life anyway to which I could escape
if I escaped this fire,
I'd live with skin that no words, nor actions
could stitch
Because who am I kidding
This world doesn't deserve a witch like me
A witch like me is the enemy
A witch like me has only one kind of a story
It begins at the edge of the town and ends in
pelting stones
I still feel them in my bones
So I'll sleep tonight, I'll sleep and dream of love
and magic
I've got a little whiff of hope under my pillow, I
won't let anyone catch it

A Desert of Magic Tricks

The sand cuts into my feet
As I walk
In a desert of magic tricks
Preying on a temporary happy ending
Too many thorns, they were part of the deal
So much blood, now I can barely feel
What made me walk this walk in the first place
But I keep walking, out of habit,
Listening
To shamans singing of this trail
To a place where no one has ever been
To a destination of ecstasy
So I drag along
In a drunken state of delightful dread
And something like music in my head
I won't heed the storm
When it wills to be heard, "I'm strong"
I'll say and continue along
Because there's a promise on my wrist
With a promise to come true
So I keep walking
Towards that promise grandiose
I'll feel it, I know
If I come too close
I'll feel it, I know

When that happiness calls
For now, I'm feeling nothing at all
But a rhythm
Steady, cheering me on
So I keep walking

Yearnings

It doesn't matter where you go if you can't see
where you're going
My steps, they waver
My lips, they waver
And I reach, hands shaking for just anything to
hold on to
~

It doesn't matter who you find, if you don't want
to be alone
The queasy feeling in my chest as my hands
grab onto big and little nothings in a dark
vastness
Trying to make something I can feel
~

It doesn't matter what you say, if no one can hear
you
I yell and yell and tell the void of my sorrows,
my desires, of the emptiness in my heart- that I
challenged was bigger than the void itself
Then again, maybe I _was_ in the emptiness of
my heart
~

It doesn't matter who you want, if there's no one
to go to

I fall down on my knees and cry smilingly at
myself, in an effort to make myself matter
To say there was someone reaching out for me,
listening to me, watching me weep and holding
me, wiping my tears and holding me, caressing
my hair and holding me, shushing my screams
and holding me, telling me it will be alright and
holding me, giving me love I'd only known in
my yearnings
And holding me.

Pandemonium

What's in your head?
When you bring forts down
And dry seas out
I've seen love run out in your heart
And died a thousand deaths trying to figure out
What's in your head.

What's on your mind?
When you sing bird songs
Ask me to sing along
And then change the tune
You pull me in and then you push me out
I've burnt a thousand songs trying to figure out
what's in your head

~
~

You ask me
What's in my head
When I push you over and over, off the edge
I say I'm trying to work it through
But I don't want your help figuring out
What's in my head.

What's in your head?
You ask, well, I wonder too
There's a sad instrument playing in my room
That I dance to with your ghost
This is the music I dance to most
I have skeletons on my bed
Asking me what's in my head.

And so I ask myself what's in my head
When I feel it come to me, that dread
So I shut them all out
Though then I can't climb out
Of my own heart
But it's a start to something safe, I say
What's in my head?
That makes this confusion feel like art
Page by page, that tears me apart
And leaves everything inside me dead
I'll let you in once I figure it out because
Whatever it is, it's still in my head

The Last One

#notapoembutstillpoetry

You've read it all
My sorrows, my cries
My child-like whining, my desires, the love in
my heart and the loathe
That's my magic, I'll tell you, and my curse
To open my heart like an exhibition for you to
come and explore
And you can love it, or hate it, look at it like it's
art, or like it's an attempt at it.

I'll stand in the middle of the exhibit, feeling like
an artist -
Scared, apprehensive, awaiting your judgement,
waiting for validation
And it can make or break me.
Oh, we've all heard the independence bs, we've
all read about confidence and about self-help
But it doesn't have more power than a stranger
looking inside you and telling you your heart
spilled beautifully, that you flowered in your
melancholy, and made them feel adventurous, or
made them feel home.

So, dear reader, if this collection of yearnings, if this rendition of the truth about me, about you and about everyone else made you feel anything at all, and you continued till here, thank you.

From the bottom of my heart.

Milton Keynes UK
Ingram Content Group UK Ltd.
UKHW020644310723
426074UK00019B/1321